REFLECTIONS ON THE ART OF HORSEMANSHIP

Reflections on The Art of Horsemanship

by

H. J. HEYER

Illustrated by

C. E. EDKINS

J. A. ALLEN & CO LIMITED

LONDON

J. A. Allen & Company Ltd
1 Lower Grosvenor Place
London S.W.1

First published 1968

SBN 85131002 8

Monophoto set in Times Roman and
printed by Smith & Ritchie Ltd, Edinburgh.
Bound in Edinburgh by Henderson & Bisset.

CONTENTS

C. E. EDKINS

PREFACE

THIS book is not supposed to be another riding manual—they are a dozen to the dime, nor is it a work on the finer arts of riding. Any attempt to improve on Xenophon, de la Guérinière or Seunig would only, at its best, produce a pointless parallel.

I am, on these pages, simply trying to express a few thoughts of my own on the subject of horsemanship.

Authors throughout the history of equitation had, apparently, very little to say about feel. Masters I was fortunate enough to be helped by, seemed to shy away from the subject, though they are evidently aware that feel must be the mainstay of all riding. Reluctance to discuss it is understandable if it involves mediocre capacities and the masters, of course, realize that to convey a thought by means of words is almost impossible.

Most likely the original meaning is lost or at least contorted. Thus the master attempting to help the scholar talks the language that is both easily set forth and understood: pure mechanics. This system seems to work satisfactorily; no more. We must not forget that the master expressing himself in terms of physical laws and mechanics presents us with a translation, the original being his thoughts.

The scholar, in turn, translates the physical "facts" again into his version of a given phenomenon. This complicated system leaves ample room for misinterpretation and explains the frequent differences of description from two equally good riders on one and the same equestrian function.

The following pages are an attempt to lead the reader, disregarding forms and mechanics, into the centre of the subject, and to encourage him to integrate with it and to demonstrate how then, skill, dexterity and efficiency develop automatically—as a by-product as it were.

To help us in our attempting to see and understand the horse from within before trying to improve on it—this is the subject of this book.

What really do we understand under Training in the classic sense? Why Training at all? Is not the horse at liberty a perfectly efficient functioning entity—without the interference of man? Are we so presumptuous as to believe we could improve on nature's principles and systems? Certainly not! The laws of evolution—weeding out and tentatively testing new directions of development, controlled quantity and quality, the changing environment—demand adaptability and prevent stagnation.

Hence we can assume the sole purpose of training the horse is to make it perform its natural gaits and jumps under the rider—to the rider's command.

And where do the gymnastics come in? Nature provides all its children with gymnastics in the disguise of play. The foal's gambols and pranks are exercises. The piaffes, pirouettes, levades and caprioles it performs when in good spirits are the most ingeniously devised exercises for physical and mental fitness—so essential for survival. They are more effective than any practice designed by self-assured "Trainers" could ever be. What is more: they are so pleasant and enjoyable to do!

The thinking rider learns his lesson from nature. He, too, uses those various forms of gambols observed in the paddock to better his horse's physique and prepare it for life. He uses the authentic methods prescribed by nature, avoiding drudgery, resistance and discontentment.

And how do we go about this task, precisely?

Before setting out to train a horse, let us consider what we are actually striving for. We want to mould a living being into a mount that is as the book says, obedient, supple and trained to fitness and well-being. It is obvious that all these conditions are present in any horse before a human hand has touched it. With one exception: obedience.

This line of thinking leads us to the assumption that all we have to do in schooling a new mount is to teach it to obey our commands. But experience soon, and definitely shows the pathetic results.

A mechanical robot that has been conditioned to go through certain fancy gaits, like a wound-up clock, a machine that most likely would bust a few springs were it asked to perform a dressage test in reverse, a freak useless to and for anything but its learned tricks. A most unhappy creature. The product of human folly.

It is clear to us that we can never recreate those graceful, unconstrained, and happy movements and jumps of the youngsters in the paddocks by means of obedience-education. The reason for this is simply the shortcomings of man who had to be God to be able to pull all those hundreds of strings at the right time and rate to make a job of it.

To reproduce a true replica of the recognised example—the horse at liberty—we can take only one way. We make use of what is left of these original qualities, after the shock of being saddled and mounted, and build up on it.

We feel our way into the pulsating movements of life itself, offering friendship, expecting nothing in return.

Imprinted in our mind is the ideal we are sure to accomplish sometime in the future: The horse-rider combination becoming a near one-unit reality.

The horse will approach us sooner or later for help and then—only then—do we become active, communications commence—training starts.

All this of course requires a great deal of skill and tact and feel, a degree of feel which could probably be better called intuition.

Let us now go back to that paddock to study the prototypes nature provided us with. Let us examine those movements and jumps through the eyes of a sculptor visualising his model.

We now see action and its results in a very different way.

For example those sudden halts after a fast move-

Sudden halt . . .

ment provide us with a wealth of thought, as to how the terrific strain on the forelegs and shoulders is greatly reduced by flexing the haunches and stepping forward with the hindlegs.

We observe that horses prefer the turn on the haunches to turning on the forehand. It is quicker, safer, the field of vision unobstructed and the readiness for instant take off not impeded. The horse only performs turns on the forehand out of necessity when anchored by the head through halter and rope.

We further see contra shoulder-in along a fence, a passage of an agitated youngster or stallion, flying changes, strong trot with greatest impulsion, galloping from the halt, and if we stay for long enough we might see the classic curbettes of two mock fighting youngsters—to the benefit of the girls of course—and we might even be presented with a capricious jump for joy; the capriole.

We study this all thoroughly, try to absorb the atmosphere and let ourselves be absorbed by it. We try to feel the moods for which there are no words but which express themselves in actions. But we must refrain from paying too much attention to pure mechanics.

Technicalities necessitate analysing, which once started send us through a process of chain reactions producing only question marks or a collection (incomplete) of parts (distorted) which certainly do not resemble a horse.

In training, a horse can only be treated as a whole. One cannot exercise one part without affecting others.

First attempt at a pirouette

We leave the paddocks when we feel enriched by the experience of having seen life itself, having felt something about the greatness of it and come a little closer, almost in touch with the divine meaning of it.

Having thus acquired a clear mental picture of natural and therefore classic movements we are now well prepared and fortified to approach the next chapter, i.e. we will mount and try to actually feel the pulsating life, get accustomed to rhythm, balance, and rate; acquire subconsciously a feel for temperament, moods and character.

The medium of contact is the seat. Through the seat we give and take, receive and transmit.

An enormous amount of verbiage spoken and printed, has been and will be devoted to the seat wherever horses are saddled. However, most discussions deal with the How rather than the Why and as in most technical discussions and disputes, analysis creeps in, destroying the whole structure which, again, is a wholesome one and must be treated as such.

It is a grave mistake to show a scholar an example and ask him to copy it. The seat is determined by the horse and as many horses there are so many seats are there.

The classic seat is not an invention to satisfy fashion or pride of achievement.

The classic seat is simply a by-product of good riding, or better: it is the only seat possible when riding within the classic context. i.e. The rider who aims to be able to be *with* the horse continuously and in all movements:

> will be unconstrained (passive) and supple (active);

Unconstrained balance, supple contact

. . . who tries to avoid disturbance and endeavours to achieve horse-rider-oneness;

will be in perfect balance with himself and his horse;

. . . who sits steady and comfortably, is able to feel readily and enjoys continuous and effortless communication with his horse;

will have the greatest possible contact area with his horse;

and will find himself automatically in the classic seat.

The rest is determined by the horse's grade of development. With increased flexion of the haunches and development of the stretcher muscles on the rib-cage the stirrups will have to be lowered. And the rider's slightly forward leaning upper body on a raw horse will come more back to and past the vertical as the horse's collection increases, appropriate to and in accordance with movement and flexion.

Let us imagine the seatbones are the pivot of the whole mass—horse with rider. Now the rider goes in the forward driving-seat. He braces his back, pushes his pelvis forward-down towards the withers; his legs lengthen, heels down to the ground, calves "breathing" with the pulsating barrel, shoulders slightly more back. This will tilt the whole mass back: hindlegs reach farther forward, haunches flex and lower the croupe; forehand enlightened. This is the classic forward-driving seat and only grade of intensity, slight twist of shoulders and shift of hips, an indication of banking or a feather-light turn at the wrists will make the difference between a passage or a strong trot, a turn, lateral flexion, gallop left or right, pirouette or flying change, a levade or a strong gallop. This classic seat is of course only possible in a forward movement; the mass cannot be shifted nor the scale tilted without the help of impulsion.

The small of the back being the cross-roads of all messages is the part that tires first. In fact a tired back is only to the credit of the rider. The back must be elastic—not relaxed: with plenty of give in all directions, but with the definite tendency to return to zero.

We are now trotting along completely free of tension. Our horse carries itself and does not need support on the reins. The rider goes with the movement, legs are kept on the horse's sides through their own weight.

Gripping legs are tiring, prevent any feel, cannot give well measured aids and make an unsteady seat by pushing the rider away from the horse like closing scissors from a table edge. It is surprising how many riders "grip" and most don't even know it.

The remedy is to get hold of the pommel with one hand, pulling yourself forward-down, at the same time opening the legs, pushing heels out and down then bring the legs, knees first, on the horse (gently).

This gives us a very steady, deep seat; one with long legs, flat on the horse, we now have all the contact area we could wish for.

The most instructive example of this seat is the monument of Prince Eugene in Vienna.

What we must avoid is what is sometimes wrongly called the hunting seat, with short legs, toes and knees out, seat back in the saddle. Here the rider touches the horse at six points only; seat bones, thigh muscles and calves, thus preventing any feel which makes it impossible to give correctly timed and measured aids, in short, training to any worthy standard is barred.

It will be necessary for a start to correct our seat in the above-mentioned way every two minutes. As soon as we get bounced out of it, we halt, correct and proceed. After a few days we will be able to correct while trotting along and eventually without the help of the hand on the pommel.

It does then become a habit and we just do not feel right should we for some reason forget it.

This all sounds very tedious and unnecessary pedantry but we will see directly how important it is to make this steady, unconstrained, well balanced, deep seat our natural one, in as much that should we lose it, we subconsciously correct it.

Only then can we expect any results from the next stage in our development. There is a short cut for acquiring a feel for all the mysteries going on under the saddle:

Having the privilege to sit on a well-trained horse executing a few school movements, with a master telling you what to do, namely: nothing!

On a horse of mediocre standard it takes longer, but the principle is the same. Here again the motive is: do nothing, and more important still: think nothing.

We empty our heads completely, creating a vacuum to make room for impressions.

We forget about legs, shoulders, muscles, reins and what have you (we might have to close our eyes to be able to), and try to catch some of those messages, sent out unceasingly, which went past unnoticed so far because we were too busy thinking about our knees or hands.

Let us imagine that we are standing at the beach, waist deep in water, facing the shore, again with closed eyes. The surf sweeping up at us from behind makes us very uneasy.

The waves throw us off balance, the sea is master of the situation, playing with us, simply because we are not part of it and because of our resistance to going with it.

After a while (with eyes still closed) we get used to the surf, its timing and force, and we now begin to enjoy it, we open our eyes and go with the movement, becoming so confident that we wish for bigger waves.

We intensify our going with the movement as if to push the waves up higher, sending them further on the beach.

And as the wave runs out on the sand and is on the verge to return, we catch it with our hands, ever so lightly bring it back through our arms shoulders and back to where it came from to "push up" the next one with our back and our hips, like a child on a swing.

If we now interrupt our dream of the beach, we will realize that we have just started to train our horse.

By pushing up that wave we have created a force which we have allowed to roll out forward and caught it only at the very last moment to bring it back to create another one.

In terms of equitation this means we have picked up the hind legs, brought them forward under the mass, aided the wave of energy forward with our forward driving seats, the "giving" wrists let out a long forward stride, catching the flow of energy at the last moment. The principle of all training.

As the surf of the beach, every stride of the horse will be slightly different in force, speed and timing.

What ever we do to correct it we first have to create that extra impulsion; then, and only then, can we force it in either a forward extension or collection with all the myriads of nuances between.

Aids

The definition of aids is to help, helping as opposed to commanding.

Helping the horse towards more and easier efficiency, creating a measured amount of energy and helping the waves of energy along, directing them to wherever they are needed or wanted. In the classic sense aids—any aids—are based on reactions: the rider's aids cause reactions and are in turn produced through reactions.

Let me explain here that the term classic is not limited to Haute Ecole exclusively but can be safely extended to include any riding executed perfectly, or near perfectly, within the basic laws of nature. That is to say:

(1) Making the whole horse do the job more easily by means of thorough preparation through gymnastics, and

(2) Perfecting co-ordination and co-operation to a level where the horse-rider team approaches the one unit status.

The quality of training at the Spanish Riding School in Vienna and the results it shows are the outstanding example of an ideal and how this ideal can be achieved.

But classic riding can also be observed; on Show-jumping courses, or in cattle corrals in some parts of the world, mainly Mexico.

There are two schools of thought regarding training; teaching the horse and training through reaction.

What speaks against teaching is, first of all its superficiality, which the horse will discard to fall back on its more reliable instincts, at the slightest sign of approaching emergency or doubt in the value of the learnedness.

A taught horse is unsafe, most unco-operative, extremely tiring for the rider whose conscious mind has to click continuously and it performs like a wound-up robot.

It is impossible for any rider to know of all the functions and influence them. Therefore the system of teaching the horse is doomed to mediocrity before it starts. How, then, can we communicate with our horse? How can we stimulate it, coax it, to accept our leading and aiding through gymnastics, how do we establish contact?

To find the answer let us examine a green horse and try to find out how it reacts.

Let us assume it dozes in the shade of a tree, its mind far from training, in fact such thoughts are unknown to it.

Let us further take it that our guinea pig is a placid one and we can touch it without causing alarm. If we now put a twig lightly to the lower part of the ribs, one or two things will invariably happen; the horse's same-sided hind foot and/or its nose will move towards the point of annoyance.

A nudge of another horse or a fly landing at this very spot will cause the same reaction. So will, later during training, the rider's leg.

In other words a leg aid can pick up a hind leg, flex a horse and during progressive training, control timing, impulsion, flexion, cadence and animation.

In contrast to general belief, leg aids are not forward driving aids.

One can teach the horse with the help of whip and voice that leg pressure means forward and the obliging horse will, no doubt, obey, if only to get away from those hammering legs which are by no means "aiding" the horse but annoying it. In fact the rider kicks the horse away from himself—physically and spiritually—instead of aiming for the one-unit-ideal.

The only forward driving aid is a collection of several co-operating aids, which we call the forward driving-seat, where the knees and heels push down towards the ground with the legs gently "breathing" with the horse's movements, and the seat and pelvis pushing forward-downwards against the withers.

A lot has been said and written about the timing of aids. The controversy is most confusing to the scholar, as most renowned experts seem to contradict themselves and each other.

To solve the problems let us again ask the sole authority: the horse.

The rider who has acquired a classic seat will, without any difficulty, feel when, and later with experience, how the hindlegs move. The contractions and relaxations of the muscles under his calves pulsating in rhythm with the strides cause the rider's lower legs to be pushed away and allowed to fall on the horse, the falling-on resulting in a gentle tap.

This slight tap is the proper timing for any leg aid, in fact it is in itself a leg aid, influencing the next stride of the same-sided hind leg. Very helpful for the rider going through this lesson is a well-trained horse, moving in a collected trot, or better, piaffe.

We feel the constant to and fro of messages and answers. Aids causing reactions and reactions causing aids.

One well performed canter stride requires about 1 dozen aids with ½ dozen possible ones. The stride does not take more time than say, a car driver requires to switch from "drive" to "brake" in an emergency. Our driver has in this short time lag only to apply two "aids": shift his foot from the gas to the brake pedal and wrestle with the steering wheel. In many cases even these two aids are not performed well enough, or not at all, or there would be fewer accidents.

How now can a rider execute 1 to 1½ dozen aids at different timing with varying intensities and only determined shortly before this canter stride commenced, some even necessitated during the stride. It is only possible through automatic and subconscious reactions.

The button pusher and puller will always be too late and only disturb the horse in its balance and natural flow of movement; why not ride therefore with the help of subconscious reactions. There is no time lag, they are reliable and it leaves the mind free and uncluttered, the latter probably being the eminent part. A mind blocked by theories and technical conceptions cannot work freely and efficiently, just as a constricted muscle somewhere will block the flow of energy. Let me repeat, even at the risk of boring, analysing and separating the diverse aids for a given movement can only end in confusion.

Authors of books on riding generally lose themselves by endeavouring to describe the various aids necessary to perform say, a shoulder-in. The scholar who tries to reconstruct the shoulder-in by following

Jarring disharmony

The classic halt

the above mentioned author's four hundred words blue-print will find his mount happily grazing in the neighbour's paddock, while he is only halfway through his count down.

Our scholar would obtain much quicker and better results if he was asked simply to bank himself with the mount as if he wanted to turn a corner on a bicycle, simultaneously concentrating on a more expressed forward-driving seat with the emphasis on the inner hindleg which now has to flex more.

The rider is now not a remote control button pusher any more but becomes part of the system. Instead of watching a register of knobs and levers to be pushed and pulled, the rider sees his horse and himself as one unit, performing happily and seemingly effortlessly, thanks to a 100% automatic intercommunication system, whose efficiency improves progressively with training—again—automatic.

Let me quote here the Maître Oliveira "caress the horse to go forward". In this age of automated riding and, let us admit it, the classic art's lowest standard ever: this master presents us with this jewel: caress the horse to . . .

This is the essence of all training and explains its meaning in the shortest and most precise way.

We who refuse to bludgeon the horse into obedience, who discarded education as inefficient, we caress the horse to accept us and include us in an already perfect system. To caress the horse to go forward is the ultimate answer to all queries and is indeed one of greatest wisdom of life. It is as old as early Hindu myths and Lao-Tse's writings. But it is this precious combination of philosopher, poet and master horseman, Oliveira, who opens our eyes to the fact that it, too, is the foundation of the classic art of riding. Let us meditate on it whenever we are in the saddle: Caress the horse to . . .

Training

THE QUESTION arising first when considering training or, for that matter horsemanship in general, is: What is good and what is bad?

To put it as short and clear as possible, one can say good horsemanship is when a horse-rider combination comes as near as possible to performing as one unit. The object being a fluent co-operation, unconstrained and with a happy disposition.

To train the horse, or in better words, prepare it through gymnastics, for a better and easier performance it is essential to have a good communication system.

The reason for training is mainly to prepare the horse through gymnastics to extreme fitness. To begin with we make it easier for the horse by putting the whole animal to work.

This sounds perplexing, but let us have a good look at a rather green horse under a rider. The forelegs carry the forehand and two thirds of the middle-hand and the rider. The hind legs, against that, only push. The muscles of the hind quarters though designed for bigger capacity, are neglected and undeveloped.

Let us now compare this green horse with one that has been trained for three years by a master of the Spanish School.

Here we see a horse that makes use of all its body to do the job on hand. There is not one muscle, tendon, sinew or joint that does not contribute to any movement. Even a layman does get the impression that this horse can, when called on, do anything with ease and grace, longer, and do it happily; and in fact this horse will go all day, jump six feet without an obstacle and continue doing so to the age of thirty or more.

The Vaqueros of Mexico, who train their horses on the same line, do not have to change horses during a day's hard work of cutting out cattle. The world's top jumpers put a considerable amount of ground work in the line of classical training before tackling jumps and if one studied the individual cases one finds a striking evidence of how intensive and timely extended dressage before attempting to jump, results in longer lasting success, in international show jumping events.

These two or three years spent in classical training do pay dividends in the long run and the so-called rider who prepares his horse for whatever it will be required to do by just "feeding it fit" and then goes hell for leather does not come up to competitive standard with his product, not in quality, nor physical fitness, nor beauty, nor endurance and longevity.

Let me draw your attention to the Charros and Vaqueros of Central America who train their horses thoroughly and with great thought to a degree where school movements are, in a matter-of-fact way, self evident—as a means to work cattle efficiently and to enjoy themselves—*with* their horses.

Let us further remember that the stallions of the Vienna Riding School are systematically trained to a perfection where they jump five feet without an obstacle and this in slow motion, proving the enormous strength available.

These movements are natural, the reproduction of the foal's frolics, and must therefore find any horse's and any genuine horseman's approval.

From the materialistic point of view there are enormous advantages for any specialised riding purposes, may it be stock work, polo, jumping or training the scholar. One more argument for our case; riding and training a horse in advanced school movements brings out man's noble qualities.

The Duke of Newcastle gives it to us more bluntly. But instead of losing our way in philosophy, let us take another example.

The two axemen, No. 1, the pen pusher, whose only physical exercise consists of mowing the lawn on Saturday, decides to chop a few sticks for the barbecue. He uses two arms, two shoulders and half a back to swing the axe. Result: sore muscles for three days and a depressed mind as "the old bones don't seem to be good any more".

This chap's counterpart, the professional axeman swings his axe all day long, never getting sore or tired, and how graceful and easy it looks! He swings from the tip of his toes, a wave of energy going through the whole body down to his hands delivering the blow.

Being convinced of the importance of developing

the whole horse we start our gymnastic training, by stimulating and encouraging the hindlegs to tread forward under the mass, to flex and willingly carry more of the load.

This will relieve the shoulders and forelegs of some of their burden enabling them to move freer and easier, imperative for both collected and extended movements.

The mass of horse and rider becomes easily balanced between the rider's aids and further gymnastic exercises like transitions and longitudinal flexions will make the horse supple and strong.

Obedience is an often discussed concept, and any dressage judge will readily explain that it is obedience he is primarily looking for. (But let us not forget that a 100% obedient horse can only have a dictator on top of him.)

This is often misunderstood and it is probably the word obedience that causes all the unclassic schooling and teaching methods.

Horses training and ridden with reaction-causing aids are "automatically obedient" but in a much differing way to the trained dog. Moreover this trained horse will willingly accept rider's guidance, instinctively realising the advantage of physical fitness as an essential to happiness.

Training, or let us use that misleading word just this once, dressage, is therefore simply the physical and mental preparation for a job not as yet decided.

Whatever the rider plans to specialise in later, the first basic training will have to be the same, and the longer and more intensive the first training is done, the quicker and easier the results later.

But all training, whatever the purpose, Haute Ecole, jumping, hunting or stock work, will only show results and therefore be of any value, if based on unconstrainedness.

The trainer's first aim is to "show the way down", with his hands, which will bring the back up to its natural position. The gently driving seat encouraging the horse to reach forward with his nose, the reins, letting the strides out, only keep a very light contact.

The second part of training, the proper gymnastics (flexing and bending) should not be introduced to the horse until it carries itself free and unconstrained in all paces. Let me take the classic example.

The young stallions in the Spanish School, Vienna, are for the first year only ridden "forward with a free-swinging back" unconstrained and with aiding to better balance.

In the second year, the rider increasingly engages the hindlegs and through various exercises supples and strengthens the horse simultaneously.

With the horse getting stronger and more and more supple, developing a finger-tip controlled balance. In the third year we then see the dainty flying change, majestic piaffe and passage, graceful pirouette and powerful strong trot.

The show jumper will have branched off before this, though it would have done his horse a lot of good if he kept going.

There is no better body-building exercise than the piaffe.

But we are now entering the world of art, the art of modelling a living creature. Not everybody can be an artist and it is not everybody's call to attempt the utmost, possible perfection, but every rider can be horseman enough to give his mount a good basic preparation for life.

So let us discuss a few basic rules for training; it is, of course, as we are dealing with a living creature, very dangerous to stick to rules and nothing hampers progress more than preconceived ideas and methods; planning is definitely "out".

We cannot discuss the individual situations, but we can safely set up a few general hints.

This is not a book on how to train a horse, there are several very good ones available,* I only want

* W. Museler, *Riding Logic*.
W. Seunig, *Horsemanship*.
G. Steinbrecht, *Le Gymnase du Cheval*.
F. R. de la Guérinière, *Ecole de Cavalerie*.
Xenophon, *Art of Horsemanship*.

to express a few ideas I have not seen published or heard spoken of as yet.

It is my personal experience that no, or very little, results are achieved by planning the development of certain movements, the overcoming of difficulties or programming a course of training. If I may very much generalise things: one starts with the ordinary and progressively advances on two parallel lines, one towards collection, the other, forward impulsion.

Thinking in terms of trot, at the end of one line (an optical illusion, it is not really the end), piaffe and levade; the other line leads to the strong trot. Collection and extension help developing each other and in classical terms one is unthinkable without the other.

Free moving and enlighted shoulders and forelegs in a strong trot are only possible through flexed haunches and hindlegs treading well forward and under the weight of the mass.

On the other hand, an unconstrained, animated and free swinging and well balanced collected trot can only be executed by the horse that has learned to move forward, easily and free.

It is rather futile to work with determination on, say, the flying change. Time and patience are the main helpers to "get there" with much better and, most important, lasting results.

The horse that has been prepared through pure gymnastics and a near perfect communication system to canter well cadenced, in perfect balance, will only have to feel the rider's hip shifting slightly to make it change legs.

If the horse: rider relationship is well enough

established and the communication system brought to near perfection the time will come when the rider no longer adjusts himself to the horse but the horse follows the rider. (Thus eventually to a degree where the rider turning his head will automatically turn the horse.)

All classical movements of dressage and High School develop automatically. This is easily understood when we realise that our horse has mastered this long before we put the saddle on him, in the paddock as a joyfully playing youngster.

The rider whose main aim during training is the approach and advance towards the horse and rider—one unit ideal—this mainly through developing the communication system cannot fail having results.

The greatest mistake is to consider and actually treat this communication system as a one-way traffic. In fact, the endless chatter between horse and rider starts with horse sending and the rider receiving; pity the rider who has his set turned off.

There are myriads of horse to rider messages which must be answered and it is the ability to receive and answer these messages that distinguishes the naturally gifted rider from the "would-be".

At the same time, he sends his messages, and here again it is the good rider who perceives the echo they produce which will in turn partly determine his next signal. It is obvious that the human brain is not efficient enough to deal with this immense traffic with its conscious mind through reasoning.

Only reflexes and subconscious reactions can cope with the job. The pulsating muscles under the rider's legs cause these to give slight "breathing, feathering" taps, encouraging the hindlegs to tread forward and under, thus putting the rider in the deep forward driving seat which in turn, now balances the whole mass. Let us for a moment listen to this horse and rider chatter:

R. How about a canter sleepy?
H. Good idea: there, how is that?
R. No good. We must do it together, you know.
H. All right, you say when.
R. Well, I suggest we canter on the right, O.K. with you?
H. Yes. Yes. Go ahead.
R. Now then, balance us properly, good, your left leg forward under the mass. Flex it, damn you, we are now both sitting on that leg.
H. But this is hard work. Oh, boy, you are heavy.
R. Never mind, your right hind and fore are now free to move forward and up. Do so.
H. Hm.
R. Quite good. Now push off with your left hind: hey, not too jerky, you clown.
H. Boy, this is fun.
R. Don't fall on your nose; bring those hindlegs forward.
H. Don't pull on my mouth stupid.
R. Sorry. Better now?
H. Passable. But stop bouncing about, will you?
R. Hey, you cheat, bring that big behind of yours in and flex your haunches.
H. Happy now?
R. Very, thank you.
H. This is good fun. Nearly as good as two years ago in the paddock.

R. Yes, only don't bend so much. Bring this left hind more forward, yes that's good.

H. Break it up, slave driver; I'll be stiff and sore all over, tomorrow.

R. You're right. Once more only. Bring those hind-legs of yours more forward. Both, stupid.

H. Stupid yourself, balance yourself better.

R. Sorry. Balance yourself and me on those hind-legs, good, come down gently on your fore. No, not forward, relax your hindquarters. Yes, quite good. Thank you very much.

The rider who rides his horse with his forward driving seat mainly, encourages it to use all his available muscles, sinews and joints to do a better job easier, who chatters with his horse endlessly and aims for the one unit ideal, will one day be presented with a few tentative passage steps though he was only trying to perfect the collected trot.

At another occasion, cantering on two tracks, the horse might offer the beginning of a pirouette, or a more intensive collection in the piaffe, will produce the most glorious of all school movements, the levade.

These offerings by the horse are proof of good classic training as a well trained horse is the best instructor, so it is, too, the best judge of its own training.

Movements

GENERALLY speaking, the movements, figures and paces discussed hereunder are, more or less, gymnastic exercises and as such part of the training system.

They are all natural movements, familiar to the horse, though the style will of course be somewhat cramped in the earlier stages of training. As the development of these exercises progresses to a matter-of-course perfection, one can regard the process of training a successful one.

Not satisfied with this, the perfectionist goes further, towards the 99·9% mark and by doing so will be presented by his horse, with glorious school movements, on and later above the ground.

Blessed is the rider who reaches these heights. Is it worthy to go so far? It depends whether the question is an economic or a philosophical one. Everyone has to decide it for himself according to his convictions.

But, no-one should attempt to use a horse, in whatever form it might be, hunting, jumping, stock work, polo, military, without training it first to a stage where it can take the strain easily, saving itself and the rider a lot of misery and annoyance.

There is no substitute for thorough systematic training. It is only fair to give the horse that carries us a chance to develop itself to do so.

Walk, trot, gallop

NUMEROUS good books, some of unsurpassing excellence, have been written on horsemanship in general and the development of gaits in particular.

It would be ridiculous to attempt to improve on them, but I would like to clarify a few points of uncertainty that seem to have crept in to stay.

In the walk, the sequence of legs is a decidedly more intricate one than in the trot. Some old masters follow the principle that the trot develops the walk and the walk the gallop. This truth is still valid and it surprises me to see so many trainers introduce new movements first in the walk.

What helps the horse to overcome initial difficulties in the progress of training is mainly forward impulsion. That alone decides hands down for the trot, as the principle pace against the walk.

The comparatively simple sequence of the legs, too, decides in favour of the trot for most exercises, especially so in the early stage of training. The working trot is what we begin with. We develop it to a quality where one can use it as a working basis. From the working trot, we develop the collected trot and from there via the middle the strong trot.

Transitions hold the whole structure together; they are as important as any one of the paces.

Before the rider sets off in the trot (or walk, or gallop) he should decide at what rate he wants to go and then stick to it.

What one generally sees, unfortunately, is a joggling sort of mess which is neither this nor that. The reason for this muddle is, I think, ignorance of the riders and not necessarily lack of skill.

There are four distinct trots the rider should endeavour to keep separated: the working, collected, middle and strong trot; in that order.

Walk

The Walk is the most neglected of all movements and one very rarely sees a good walk performed by an otherwise well developed horse. The walk is no spectacular movement and most likely not exciting enough for younger riders, though a well balanced walk with cadence and measured impulsion giving the impression of great power reserve and pleasant well-being is a beautiful experience, for rider and spectator alike.

The step-child status of the walk creeps in at the early stage of training. One gives the horse a spell during the daily training session, letting everything go, allowing the horse to relax. The precious contact is lost only to be found again, generally a tedious endeavour—when the lesson continues.

A silly and apparently incurable habit indeed! The horse would appreciate this spell much more if kept on the aids with communication system intact. To give the horse a well earned breather from muscular exertion, it is much more effective to walk with long easy-flowing strides than let everything fall to pieces, pieces that are a lot of bother for horse and rider to assemble again.

There is no sense in throwing the reins away altogether except perhaps for the less experienced rider, in order to determine whether his mount carries itself.

If, and when, we want our horse to relax completely, we unsaddle and groom it, put it in its paddock or yard or stable and feed and water it; the riding arena is the gymnasium of the horse, not a recreation centre.

One hour's work is not too much for any horse and can easily be put up without relaxation spells. This hour's exercise will be evenly interspersed with three or four walk sequences which require less muscular exertion and constitute a pause in themselves. But the walk should always be considered a movement to be worked on as any other movement.

We have to keep in mind a distinct difference between the long walk, with roomy ground covering and rather flat strides, the middle or working walk and of course the collected walk. All three have their practical purpose and should be treated that way. For covering distance it is the long walk we choose. But it has to be developed in the riding arena, in short sequences.

The stepping out well forward with a comparatively long neck and the hindlegs well supporting is the object.

The collected walk is obviously the one in which we introduce new movement and figures as exercises. Here the hindlegs are encouraged to step more forward under the load, the action becomes higher, fore and aft and as the haunches flex more the centre of gravity moves back, enlightening the forehand and the movement gets more animated but not quicker.

As in the trot we develop the collected walk and the long walk contemporary, as here, too, one develops the other and one is not possible without the other. And here, too, it is the transitions that will be most beneficial in developing towards the two extremes; the long forward movement and collection.

Shoulder-in

One of the most important gymnastic exercises for developing the horse is the shoulder-in. Properly executed it helps to make the horse supple, develops its poise and strengthens its haunches, shoulders and back.

The longitudinal flexion is a tonic for the back muscles and furthers the pliability of the ribcage; the inner hindleg, encouraged to step well forward under the mass, enlightens the outer fore of some of its burden, enabling the latter to move free and easy which in itself is an excellent help in developing the strong trot.

It is important that the horse carries itself. Bearing down on the bit and resisting longitudinal flexion prove that the hindlegs are not engaged properly and that we have asked too much to begin with. The weight is evenly distributed over the four legs, but the "banking", the intensity of which is determined by degree of flexion and rate, lowers the inner side, mainly the hip. Consequently the inner hindleg must flex more if the cleanness of the movements is to be maintained.

Shoulder-in

This increased flexion spells more work for this inner hindleg in comparison with the outer and relative to the outer foreleg is enlightening.

The shortening of the inside hindleg is of course very slight and hardly visible but easily felt through the seat.

Lowering the horse's inner hip will have the same overall effect as the shortening of a back leg of a chair by say half an inch and shifting one's weight on to this shorter leg; the diagonal opposite will come off the ground.

Our horse's outer fore must therefore be relieved of at least some of its burden, encouraging it to play its muscles freely, which means gymnastic exercises and preparation for those high and graceful actions, as well as forward reaching, ground gaining strides in all movements.

The rider's legs pick the hindlegs up with emphasis on the inner leg which, as said before, has to flex slightly more and is under greater strain. The rider's shoulders and outer leg regulate the longitudinal flexion, the driving-seat keeps up impulsion, back and hands maintain balance. His weight is pulled somewhat into the concave side of lateral bend.

A great deal of feel and finely measured aids are necessary to keep the movement cleanly flowing. The whole rider-horse mechanism balances on the rider's inner seat bone, so to speak, and it is the rider's sensitivity and delicately applied aides that keep it there. It is obvious that only having to flex one hindleg pronouncedly (in comparison to two on the straight) the rider can very easily ask too much of his horse.

As in all training, but especially so in the development of the shoulder-in it is wise rather to ask too little than too much, qualitatively and more so even quantitatively.

Six strides—left and right—as well performed as the horse can comfortably do it with the rider putting his whole self to the task to help is all that is required to ensure steady and certain progress. The horse will offer all it safely can if the rider is sensitive and sensible enough to recognise the limit before it is reached.

Gallop

THE gallop is for the beginner a more comfortable movement than the trot, due to the swing-like motion. It ranges from the very collected, almost on the spot, school gallop, to the so-called hunting gallop.

We begin with the working gallop and work towards collection and forward impulsion concurrently. The leading motive throughout the training period is—on a sixty by twenty metres arena—to put the emphasis on collection on the short sides, increasing progressively flexion of haunches, encouraging the hindlegs to step under, enlightening the forehand with subsequent higher action. The stored up energy is then—going through the second corner, increasingly transformed into forward impulsion by progressively lengthening the strides—without losing flexion of haunches and just before the next corner—first of next short side—we catch the forward impulsion, converting it into collection again by asking the hindlegs to step more forward while the hands catch the forward moving energy just before dead centre, so to speak, at each stride.

A succession of half parades over several strides,

the number of which are determined by the horse's standard of development. Numerous exercises can be undertaken in the gallop, all beneficial to the horse's development. In some cases the trainer might be able to overcome difficulties with the help of the more pronounced impulsion of the gallop, he was unable to master in trot or walk, and he is well advised to make full use of it. After all it will make the horse's and his work a lot easier.

Every horse has as we all know a natural curvature one way or another and during all gallop exercises it is very advantageous to put more emphasis on the difficult side. The horse gallops slightly bent around the rider's inner leg and due to the order in which the horse's legs move in the gallop it has a greater chance to correct curvature in the gallop than in other movements. Let us examine the sequence of leg action in the gallop more closely. To strike off from a halt to gallop say leading right the horse brings its left hindleg forward towards the centre of gravity to support the whole mass. The forelegs and right hindleg are now free to reach forward while the left hindleg provides the necessary thrust. We need not go any further for the time being to understand how to facilitate a strike-off to gallop with our aids. Still concerned with striking-off leading right. (1) Our left leg behind the girth, right hip forward and weight tending to the right cause a slight longitudinal flexion. (2) Our left leg encourages the horse's left hindleg to go forward under the mass. (3) Energetic forward-driving seat with emphasis on right hip causes the jump-off while the hands yield sufficiently to allow the horse to jump forward. A half parade then gathers the horse in preparation for the next stride and the whole procedure is repeated at each successive stride. It is important that the aids are applied in one fluid sequence, smoothly and in fact partly overlapping to avoid disturbance and erratic action.

This all appears to be extremely complicated but functions in fact automatically with neither the horse nor rider being consciously aware of it. The more the outer hindleg steps under to carry the load the higher the degree of collection; when virtually the whole of the mass is balancing on this leg we are almost galloping on the spot. To lengthen the strides we simply "let them out" further with shoulders and hands, but never all the way; the horse would fall to pieces, the next stride would be on the forehand, collection lost, haunches stiff and the horse supporting itself on the bit.

The flying change represents no difficulties if the horse has been prepared for it thoroughly. It is ready for it when it gallops well balanced through transitions without losing poise nor cadence, when it can strike off from the halt for two or three strides to halt again on both legs. This latter is an excellent exercise and I would like to elaborate on it.

We stand on a straight line, striking off from the halt to canter right, very slowly, well collected and with even cadence; smooth halt after six or eight strides, pause, strike off left etc. Gradually we reduce the number of strides between halts to three, two or even one. This of course cannot be achieved in weeks; to attain one stride between halts might take eighteen months. We do not have to wait that long for our flying change.

I would say a horse that canters well collected and calmly and in balance and without loss of contact with its rider in three-stride-sequences is ready for the flying change, in fact it might have offered one or two already during these preparatory exercises.

It is now the simple matter of going through this exercise without pausing for a halt. Results do come astonishingly easy if the preparation is thorough.

In fact they seem to fall into place automatically and this proves horse and rider are proceeding on classic lines.

Transitions

TRANSITIONS are the most helpful of all gymnastic exercises in training a horse.

They put, if executed well, more stress on the haunches, preparing them physically for future work.

Let us, before I go any further, visualise a perfect transition, say, from the collected trot to the strong trot and back. The horse's movement in the collected trot is well cadenced with even rhythm. Although there is impulsion to spare the horse is in perfect balance, with itself and the rider.

The rider's pulsating legs maintain cadence and encourage the hindlegs to tread forward, his seat flexes the haunches, and balances the whole mass. The weight of the reins is sufficient to maintain contact with the mouth. Should this perfect balance get lost, both horse and rider will try to re-establish the equilibrium.

To increase rate, i.e. length of stride, the rider intensifies his forward driving-seat and simultaneously "pushes" with his reins without losing contact, "letting out" every progressive stride a little more.

The increasing rate is well measured and evenly

distributed over the number of strides required for the transition. Flexion of haunches is maintained, balance not lost, impulsion still abundant, the back elastic and free. The strong trot is maintained for a few strides to assure cadence and equilibrium.

The transition back to the collected trot is performed in the same way, in fact the aids from rider to horse are with exception of reins, identical. To prevent the horse from falling on the bit the rider's seat and pulsating legs engage the hindlegs to step well under and progressively more forward to overtake the inertia of the forward impulsion, and maintain equilibrium as the strides become shorter.

Feathering rein aids, in rhythm with each stride, catch the forward flowing impulsion just before it is spent, thus preserving the energy, sending it back to its source, the haunches. Impulsion and balance are never lost throughout this exercise, flexion of haunches and lightness of the forehand are maintained. Only the length of stride increases or decreases.

Cadence does not alter, though rhythm becomes more lively at the strong trot, as the horse's feet now have to cover more distance per stride.

It is obvious that this ideal performance requires an enormous amount of physical fitness and many weeks and months, even years, of gymnastic exercises are needed to develop it.

To begin with the trainers must be contented with very slight progress, important is to maintain the quality, i.e. balance, cadence and impulsion, must not, under any circumstances be lost. No matter how small the increase of length of stride, if only half an inch for a start, the horse must not be allowed to lose equilibrium, seek support on the bit and fall on its shoulders.

This would make the exercise senseless, in fact harmful for further training. The rider's feel, or if you like intuition, must tell him to reduce again, at least two strides *before* the horse's capacity is reached. There are no better exercises than transitions and the trainer is well advised to execute them several times a day.

Besides the advantage of the physical build up for the horse, the rider's ability to sending and receiving more and more messages develops and consequently "obedience" is secured.

But let us remember that forward impulsion can only originate in collection, as a spring will only extend past zero if compressed first. Only a well-balanced horse with flexed haunches, and forward treading hindlegs willingly carrying the load can be asked to increase rate to a progressive transition.

There is no end to this fascinating lesson. Even later—much later—in the transition from piaffe to passage and back to piaffe, the job is never finished. We can only approach the near perfect. Absolute perfection can never be obtained.

It only exists in human imagination, as an example, an example worth reaching for.

Turn on the haunches and half pirouette

TURN on the haunches and half pirouette, are both excellent exercises to further the horse's development in poise and balance. Weight aids play a major part in a well executed turn on the haunches and the horse's reaction to them will improve in accuracy and promptness.

To prepare the horse for the turn on the haunches the by-far-easiest and best approach is via the half pirouette. To begin with we walk on a circle large enough to allow the horse poise, balance and correct lateral flexion with ease; the spine covers exactly the line of progress.

Now we go on a spiral, making the circle smaller and at the same time try to keep the haunches in, towards the circle's centre.

The rider's hip and legs keep the haunches in, outer leg encouraging the outside hindleg to step well forward-inwards under the mass, inner leg keeps up impulsion.

The rider's weight has a tendency towards the circle's centre, his shoulders and hands keep the forehand on the diminishing circle. This exercise has to be repeated on both hands, but must be discontinued *before* the limit of capability is reached.

After several weeks we progress steadily toward the pirouette. The transition is smooth, merely an intensified spiral.

No puzzled horse, no set backs.

The turn on the haunches differs from the pirouette as it is executed from the halt. The obvious difficulty is that here impulsion has to be created at a much greater volume to first of all set the mass in motion and then, as one leg is off the ground and the second about to leave it, the forward impulsion has smoothly but decidedly to be transformed sideways into the turn.

A good pirouette or turn on the haunches is a very advanced movement. The horse can only keep poise, balance and suppleness throughout the movement, if the hindlegs step well under and, with well flexed haunches, willingly carry two thirds of the mass.

The outer hind particularly is under enormous stress and the trainer should always remember that as it is perfection he strives for the horse has to be prepared by means of systematic gymnastics.

Moderation is the surest and quickest way to success.

One more word about weight aids. In short the horse reacts to the rider shifting his centre of gravity. We get a good example of this tendency when carrying a bale of hay. We are happiest with the bale right on top of our spine, should it shift backward forward or sideways we counteract by stepping right under it. So does the horse step under the rider. It is a natural reaction we make use of.

It must be understood though, that only slight indications of the tendency to shift one's centre of gravity will make the horse answer in the right direction. Any exaggerated leaning out of the saddle will only make the horse lean the other way. There must never be a kink in the line drawn from the rider's head to a point between the hind hoofs (seen from the back or front).

We imagine the pivot of our line of gravity is at the bottom end between the hind feet and by indicating a tendency to the left or right the whole mass answers as a complete unit.

The development of the pirouette in the gallop proceeds on a similar line as in the walk. In a way it is easier and quicker achieved, as here the increased forward impulsion can be made use of, transforming it into more collection and flexion. But impulsion must not be confused with excitement. Should the horse get excited we break the exercise off to work on something entirely different.

We put the horse through movements it knows and can easily perform till it is calm enough to approach the spiral exercises again—ever so smoothly.

A slow cadenced pirouette in the gallop is quite an achievement and here again a warning: never use it to show off or to satisfy yourself, at least not during the earlier stages of training.

The damage might be unrepairable.

Rein back

THE rein back is in the classical sense a forward movement.

The rider picks one diagonal leg pair up as if to trot from the halt, with high degree of collection. Just before the first stride approaches the one-quarter mark the rider catches the forward movement, smoothly to direct it with whatever aids he might have to use according to circumstances, back and down.

In a well executed rein back the rider must have the feel—and the spectator the impression—that the horse could and would step forward willingly and without hesitation any moment the rider choses to do so.

The test for correctness is the ability to convert a back stride into a forward one at any given moment; to move forward at any pace. It is obvious that this movement is not possible to execute in the early stages of training if we want to avoid a rein-pulling tug-of-war. A fair degree of flexion of the haunches is necessary for the horse to balance itself.

Aids must go through and the horse be supple. The rein back should not be attempted before these requirements are firmly established, and never, not at any stage of training, should the rider indulge exceedingly in rein back exercises.

The rein back is a test for the standard of general training, rather than an exercise.

The horse at liberty will only walk back if unavoidable.

I could not think of anything better to close this topic with, than old master Steinbrecht's principle: "Ride your horse forward and straighten it".

Jumping

A WORD about jumping here. The one-unit principle applies to jumping as it does to all riding, a fact that does not seem to occur (unfortunately) to a lot of sportsmen who apparently use showjumping (and their horse) as means to further their ego.

These horror pictures with riders miles off their mounts—physically and mentally—wildly galloping ponies, jerky and frantic movements, yells, bumps, grunts, whiplashing and injured horses are indeed a very lopsided affair, almost entirely in favour of the rider. All the horse gets out of this great fun is, horror, pain and general misery.

Good jumping on the other hand is a delight to watch, enjoyable to the horse and endows horse and rider with shared happiness. Horse's and rider's concentration melt into one, to a degree where co-operation becomes meaningless, as the two now act as one. The movements are fluent, smooth, and, to the spectator, graceful. One has the impression that nothing really world shaking is going on, though the horse might be jumping six or seven feet.

Graceful and light as a good ballet performance

where no notion of grunts, sighs and sweat can be taken, though the exertion must be enormous and the training to his niveau extensive.

Training a good and lasting showjumper requires skilful and patient preparation in form of gymnastics of which the first year or so on the ground is the most important stage. Only after a horse is supple enough, well balanced and generally physically developed to a degree where it can execute pirouettes, strike off in the canter from halt, perform smooth and unconstrained transitions in all paces, should it be introduced to jumping.

Here, as in all riding, it is self evident that the slower the progress the better are the results. The time "lost" during this preparation will be gained at the end—with dividends—the quality gained is beyond comparison with the wildly tearing about hit-or-miss jockey. It takes little time later and one encounters no major difficulties to raise a jump to six feet or more *if* the preparatory training was thorough.

The contemporary enthusiasm for jumping is understandable, but sooner or later the question arises: why at the cost of dressage and Haute Ecole?

Partly at least responsible are mediocre dressage judges; riders get fed up with inefficiency, greatly diverse opinions and general straw threshing. Disappointed in their fruitless search for an example, frustrated by widely differing judgments and confused by endless contradictions, they turn to jumping.

Here everybody knows the rules and has no doubt about decisions. But in this field too is an acute lack of exemplary instructors.

For example, not yet have I heard mentioned the

fact that although jumping is natural to any horse, no horse at liberty will ever jump over obstacles for sheer fun. At least I have never seen a horse hop forward and back over a log or fence and I have never heard anybody reporting such. The horse in the paddock will of course negotiate any fence, log, or creek if it wants for some reason of its own to get to the other side quickly but only if there is no other way; it will walk backwards, or stand on its head for that matter, if conditions demand it.

Were I a showjumping rider I would draw the conclusion from these facts that a great deal of ground work interspersed with the jumping, must be of great benefit to the horse's constitution, happiness and further progress. To concentrate on jumping only and solely and to disregard general gymnastic training is like developing the trot alone, forgetting walk and gallop; a one-sided unbalanced affair, senseless in itself.

Dressage competitions in Europe before the war nearly always included one or two jumps. Would it not be advisable to include some dressage in the jumping events?

But, whether the organising authorities come around to this or not, let us at least train our horses that way.

Instruction

THERE is no better instructor than the horse, preferably one well advanced in training.

It is not only a great unforgettable experience to the young scholar to be put on an accomplished school horse, piaffing between the pillars and under the watchful eye of a master, it too, is the best way to learn to sit and balance, to feel and recognise.

The advantage of using a school horse to teach pupils was known through all ages in the history of horsemanship and the old masters made full use of it.

The Spanish Riding School in Vienna continues this tradition and its results speak for themselves. These gnawing problems and uncertainties that seem to bother so many riders are solved and cleared during a school trot on the lunge in no time and for ever, and the scholar acquires at least *some* knowledge as to what to strive for when training his own horse.

However, few are the fortunate ones, so let us discuss the majority of cases. The principal aims in riding instruction are, we all agree, to train a pupil to become a good rider.

The qualities of a good rider are known to us, we

discussed them earlier. It is the instructor's job to develop them in the pupil with the emphasis on developing—not creating.

These qualities are present, more or less, in everyone, slumbering under the surface. All that remains to be done for the instructor is to arise and develop them in the proper directions.

It sounds easy, but obviously is not or there would be more good instructors. The reason for this unfortunate deficiency is as I see it the instructor's inability to see the parallel in training the horse and training the rider. Both principles are the same, namely the systematic development of reflexes and reactions into a smooth and efficiently working receiving and transmitting communication system. By means of this system the pupil will influence his horse and the horse in turn puts the rider in a proper seat causing a marked effect on the horse again, and so on indefinitely.

A ping-pong game enjoyed by both partners with, of course, momentarily, interruptions through a missed ball; but this, too, is part of the game; it happens to the very best players, only, less frequently.

We see the development of communications is the alpha and omega of our job as instructors and it will be wise to give it a lot of thought. We must under all circumstances avoid giving the pupil the impression that pushing button "A" means go, and pulling lever "B" means stop. Pure mechanics will come later, much later, as the result of experience.

For a start we make it as easy as possible for the pupil to perceive what is going on under him and receive at least some of the horse's messages. The next best means to a school horse will be a quiet, unconstrained mount (on the longe) moving in slow cadence, first in a walk then trot.

We ask the rider to be, except for the "going with the movement", passive. We restrain ourselves from talking, giving the rider a chance to concentrate on the horse.

Endlessly chattering instructors are only a nuisance and should go in for politics, they prevent more pupils from learning to ride than the internal combustion engine.

Only when we see the rider balancing naturally, his mind at ease and his body unconstrained, with the legs pulsating with the horse's movements, then—and only then—will we allow him active co-operation with the horse, encouraging him to give that slight extra tap with his lower legs, watching carefully that no constraint and stiffness creeps in. Progressively we encourage our pupil to rest his crotch against the horse's withers, i.e. forwards, downwards, but sit on the seat bones, have his legs flat but losely on the horse, his whole body pulsating with the movement, the legs beating the rhythm (not noticeable).

Degree of collection and cadence are in close relation to the pupil's progress, and it is our duty to provide the best possible conditions for the pupil. We cannot spend too much time and thought on this phase of instruction.

Its effects will be seen and felt throughout his equestrian life, paying infinite dividends. It is the foundation he later builds his own house on. Although the tower of Pisa lasted a fair time, it is certainly the exception rather than the rule—a faulty foundation is no builder's delight.

In the advanced stage the pupil is asked to intensify.

More and more signals to and from the horse are perceived, identified and put to positive use. The instructor only interferes when absolutely necessary, that is, call the rider's attention to an important signal he obviously missed, with the emphasis on horse-to-rider signals. It is a grave mistake to call the rider's attentions to his own body by trying to correct his posture.

This must prevent him from listening to his horse and only causes stiffness. The thinking instructor will find indirect ways to eliminate flaws and defects. He will, for example, correct a hunched seat by explaining the functions and aids of a parade, let the pupil execute them, lots of them. The seat will correct itself. A pulled up and stiff shoulder can be loosened by asking the rider to raise it ever further and to let it drop suddenly and them make him forget it by drawing his attention to something else, say, a dragging hindleg.

As there is no end in training, there is no end in instructing, though, later it will be on a master to master basis. No capriole is absolutely perfect, nor any master one hundred per cent accomplished; there always will be room—if only very little—for further improvement. To accept this philosophy as the meaning of life itself makes the master.

Generally we can say—as in judging—no successful instruction is possible without extensive experience in training the horse, and this is probably the reason for the lack of good instructors.

Theoretical knowledge is of very little help. I have never heard of anybody becoming an accomplished ballet dancer by means of a correspondence course, a good driver by reading books on it. Only a master can be a successful tutor, the mastership being confirmed by trained horses—masterly trained.

As far as the pupil is concerned we have nothing to say except that he be an enthusiastic horse-lover who has a serious attitude towards horsemanship. Everything else is of secondary importance. We sincerely aim for good master-pupil relationship. There can't be any progress without it. It stands to reason that the pupil approaches the master.

The instructor who has to snare pupils is no master but a job hunter.

I fully agree with Colonel McTaggart's opinion concerning the age of pupils, the Colonel claims a person under sixteen years has neither the physical nor mental capacity to ride. The minor can become a good passenger—no more. He will probably learn how to hold the reins properly but will completely miss out on receiving signals or listening to the echo of his (if any at all) aids.

These youngsters on ponies might be their parents' delight but certainly not their later masters'. During their passenger era they develop habits which are extremely difficult and time consuming to get rid of later.

My personal experience in this matter is that when I had my first tuitions from a genuine master I gave the poor wretched man much trouble and bother to undo what I thought was riding.

So, why not let the kiddies amuse themselves with swimming and tennis and assure them of better and happier equestrian activities when they are ready for it. The ponies will be thankful.

Good demonstrations should be made available to the pupil every now and then to show him the example to aim for. It's obvious that these demonstrations must be genuine and of good quality.

Here again we see that it is only the experienced trainer who can lead the way. Let us not make the mistake to analyse. Picking a flaw and trying to correct it, through demonstrations or in direct words, is useless; in fact the pupil has no hope of progress till he changes the instructor.

We must always consider (if as judge, trainer or instructor) horse and rider as one individable system. To work on the horse's neck alone in the halt (Baucher) without considering the whole horse is simply nonsense. So is the attempt say, to work on a pupil's seat without relating it to the horse's movement.

Or giving a favourable verdict to a horse who exhibits a well balanced trot with good impulsion and cadence if the tail twists to one side indicating crookedness. No part is self contained.

They all depend on each other and influence each other. If the pupil's horse is not "on the bit" we would not dream of letting him correct this with the reins. We make it clear to him that his horse's haunches don't flex, the hindlegs don't step forward the equilibrium is upset with too much weight on the forehand and forward impulsion is non-existent.

From the earliest lesson on we must strive to firmly establish the pupil's feel for the whole system. Once the pupil accepts this idea and acts accordingly he will not be shaken out of it so easily, and he will have, provided his communication system is in order and he has a sense for beauty—every possible chance to become a master himself and this is the purpose of instructing.

Judging

It is no doubt a great honour to be asked to judge a dressage competition. The judge commands an extensive authority, which, of course goes hand in hand with responsibility. This responsibility can, under certain circumstances, become very heavy; for example, at international events. A firm character and a dedication to true horsemanship that out-ranks any personal, national or political feelings are absolutely essential and must be beyond any doubt.

Positive judging without personal experience—extensive experience in both training and instructing—is not possible.

The experience in instructing gives a keen eye; the training experience prevents any doubts and pencil chewing. The ruling is unshakable and absolute, simply because this judge automatically and subconsciously puts himself in the competing rider's place.

He rides the horse, he anticipates every movement of horse and rider, gives aids and counter aids, feels actions and counter actions before the competing rider does. His comments, if only mentally, are completed and filed to be drawn on later for the verdict.

This is the ideal.

However, often outstanding judges are compelled to deliver a mediocre, let's say incomplete, judgment due to poor organisation over which he has no authority. I am thinking about lack of assistance.

For example the judge has no time to take his eyes away from the competitor to use a pencil. Nor can he watch for errors of course. His mind is fully occupied in anticipating the next step's quality, compare it with the last steps, sensing dozens of messages going to and fro and noticing their results besides actually seeing the present stride and its quality.

There is nothing supernatural about it; to our experienced judge these impressions come automatic and in the subconscious and easily as the messages he receives and sends when training and riding himself. He has an unshakable and absolute image of the standard to be judged in his mind. The pattern of a horse-rider unit trained for and performing in this particular class imprinted in his mind to be used for comparison and never to be tinkered with.

To judge a given day's standard influenced by this very day's average is detrimental and confusing to all competitors and undermines a nation's standard. We see now how important experience is. Theoretical knowledge is no substitute for it; in fact it only hinders if not derived from personal experience.

There are scores of people who swear they have seen the phenomenal personality who has never been a successful trainer but "is a great judge". This might be so but it would definitely be an exception, and I personally would prefer to be judged by an experienced and competent personality. Coming back to organisation I consider it a mistake to have a test ridden from memory because for one reason it puts the competitor to a marked disadvantage. The event becomes an intelligence or memory test. The rider, instead of concentrating on his horse—fully—has every now and then to "switch off" trying to think of what comes next.

If this "what comes next" is no problem to the rider it proves that he and his horse have learned the test, learned like the sixth grader learned a poem, to rattle it off in front of the teacher (judge).

This is just what is *not* wanted. Let me say it again even with the risk of boring you; training (dressage) is the preparation for more efficiency through gymnastic exercises. The "taught" horse's silly movements are not only extremely unattractive in their wound-up robot *quality* (a far cry from the foal's unconstrained, happy and graceful antics), they are absolutely useless in themselves and, as gymnastics, detrimental for further development.

These standard dressage tests "to be ridden from memory" are in my opinion the grave-diggers of classical training. What is so alarming is that the effects of this disorganisation are already noticeable. The remedy is more variation within the classes—dozens of various compositions can be drawn up—and the test being called during the performance.

To publish it the night before the event would only be fair to horse, rider and judge. This system would most certainly force prospective competitors to really train their horses thoroughly to the standard they plan to compete in and then exhibit whatever they might be asked to within this particular class.

In short; training (dressage) again becomes what it is supposed to be; simply gymnastics. The judge would now have the impression he could ask the competitor to ride the test back to front with equally good results, jump the enclosure, to cut out cattle and finish off with a few elaborate airs to impress one or another spectator. All within the standard of this class of course.

This is true horsemanship and the basic idea of dressage.

Some dressage test compositions are very amusing indeed, were it not for the sad results they effect on the rider and his horse, training in general and national standards. There is for instance that silly word, extended. I can never get used to it.

It automatically reminds me of a stretched out dachshund. Strong would be so much more appropriate. Novice classes are asked to rein back (!) and elementary people go around the arena in an extended (!) trot. The more advanced classes are full of fancy movements, flying changes, half passes (?), most ingeniously designed serpentines and what have you, but nobody seems to think of a clean transition for example, with the result that I have not seen one for fifteen years. For this privilege one has to go to Vienna.

I suspect the authors of those scrolls have been to circus performances too often. There should be more emphasis on simple, clean movements. A well performed transition from a clean, well balanced, unconstrained, cadenced collected trot, with animation, flexing haunches (not only hocks), willingly forward and under the mass treading hindlegs, feathering and powerful strides, the absence of crookedness, light forehand and free shoulders, feather light rein contact and the horse giving the impressions it could and would reach forward in mile-long strides any time the rider wanted it to; this little transition is in itself all the experienced judge needs to make up his mind accurately.

Simplicity and quality!

The judge's marks are his verdict. They effect the placings.

His comments affect horse and rider's further development. They are to the competitor of valuable importance, and this even more so whenever the standard is to be raised, individually or collectively.

I stated a few sentences ago the really dedicated judge has, being completely involved in the performance in front of him, no time to use a pencil. I would like to add here that even dictating is extremely distracting.

The judge has to decide whether he pays the price of missing parts of the performance for dictating *some* helpful remarks and suggestions for the competitor's benefit, or, in order not to miss anything, bring a few short explanations to paper which will not be constructive or guiding, or he clams up during the test, takes everything in, files the important points in the back of his mind, to be written down after the competitor has left the arena. Without being hurried unduly he can explain and describe the mistakes made, suggest corrective measures, indicate a path—a definite path—to be followed.

It should never be overlooked to mention, describe and explain one or two good features of a performance, no matter how mediocre.

It helps the rider to recognise and comprehend. Remarks like, "not on the bit" or "strike off on wrong leg" might be useful to the judge for later reference but are of no value to the rider, who, if he is a rider at all (which one should assume, seeing him compete) knew this himself. What he wants to know is, why? and what am I to do about it?

The competent judge gives him the answer and if he is an outstanding person he answers the questions before they actually arise. There is nothing to say about the judging itself—if an experienced trainer is at the job.

To answer the question as to what is good and what is bad, I can only repeat again and again and forever: good, is to come physically and mentally as close as possible to one unit. This is the ultimate rule to apply to horsemanship.

Let us now watch the first competitor coming down the middle line. We ignore our surroundings, with its tense atmosphere. Agitated competitors adjusting straps and chattering excitedly, officials hurrying purposely, judges polishing spectacles nervously.

The sounds of throat-clearing and car doors shutting fade off. We focus on the horse and rider approaching us. This very early phase of the test, from the entrance to the salute, can be, and generally is, a very illuminating one to the judge; the horse, being asked to advance on unfamiliar ground into a strange enclosure, stared at by a crowd, will be more or less, according to its character and temperament, distracted, disclosing a host of information to us in this field. This information will and should influence our future comments and suggestions to the rider but must not impair, under any circumstances, the markings.

The book says: "on a straight line" but let us remember that no living being can advance on an absolutely straight course. What is really meant is as near as possible to the straight. Meaning the communication system between rider and horse must be in near perfect working order. It requires a good deal of tact and feel from the rider, plus the unknown quantity: anticipation, quick and nearly almost sure responses to aids to and from the horse. Being at this stage right in front of the advancing horse we get a very clear picture of how good, or bad, horse and rider really co-operate and co-ordinate. We know, of course, that a good performance can only be achieved through gymnastics. Willingness to oblige (the expression obedience is to my opinion not quite right, it belongs to the world of teaching) will be in close proportion to suppleness, equilibrium, physical conformation, mental balance and unconstrainedness. In short, all preparatory training of horse and rider are an open book to us, to be commented on and criticised constructively.

The competing pair has now advanced closely enough for us to perceive the frame of mind both are in. We try to answer the question: Are these two happy? Are they enjoying themselves and each other? We must not neglect to have a very close look at the horse's eyes; there are untold stories to be read.

The good judge will, according to his ability, do his very best to perceive, read and comprehend as many of them as possible.

They are just as important as technicalities and, in the finer arts of riding, even more so.

Halt. Salute. Let us not get flustered. This salute is meant, not for us, but to the horse. To good horsemanship and the qualities it encloses. Art, chivalry, and friendship for the old masters who showed us the way with their example. Realising the solemnity of this salute we join in it and feel united with horses and riders all over the world. Taking part rather than sitting in judgment. This sounds paradox but is not if we realise what a confusing double misnomer "dressage judge" is.

Of course it has company, and plenty; "extension" "ordinary" "relaxed" are only some of them, though probably the most damage-causing ones. I will not comment on the test itself as I would only repeat myself. We know the example and comment accordingly, with the emphasis on *constructive* criticism.

To allow the top six or so riders of a given class to show their horses together for a certain time span, ad libitum, is an advantageous arrangement, especially in advance classes.

The rider, now freed from compulsory and predetermined executioned movements will most probably show the more extreme positive and negative points of his own ability as well as his horse's stage of training. This facilitates the final placing and provides additional food for thought for comments, which in turn is of benefit to future training.

Judges should, after the results of the competition are out, make themselves available to the competitors for discussion.

This clears the atmosphere, should it be sticky. It

provides the rider with further knowledge and gives the judge a chance to explain his markings and comments.

It can clarify misunderstandings. It shows the goodwill on both sides and guarantees further co-operation of both parties' willingness to carry the good intentions further, towards and in the sense of good horsemanship.

History and development of riding

Mongolian horseman

RIDING styles and subsequently training methods developed on two distinguished lines from the early antique one.

In the wide expanses of Asian steppes and the deserts of North Africa and the Middle East it was, and still is, of utmost importance for the rider to cover as much ground as possible to reach far away pastures or battlefields. It was (and is) a question of survival to ride a horse fast over long distances.

The essence of horsemanship here is to make it as easy as possible for the horse. Short stirrups and the rider's upper body forward into the now very much advanced centre of gravity, thus enlightening the back and leaving the hindlegs free for what is in this case so important: thrust.

There is no argument against this means of speedy transport, in fact it is natural and therefore right wherever steppe or desert conditions prevail.

The Cossacks in Southern Russia, the Csiko's of Hungaria and the Gauchos in the Pampas adopted this long and fast riding as suitable for their requirements and conditions. The results are spectacular and convincing.

One only has to experience an attacking squadron of Cossacks—even in the age of machine-guns and atom bombs—or watch the Czikos rounding up a mob of fast two year olds to be convinced that this type of riding is unconditionally the right and fitting one in its natural environment: the steppes and deserts.

A quite different style of riding however, was developed as a result of study of the horse's conformation.

The early Greeks observed that the horse's hindlegs are much stronger than the fore, though they only seem to carry one third of the mass. Being recognised as the inventors of reasoning they argued: why not make strong hindlegs take more of the load to make it easier for the whole horse?

Especially as we don't have to gallop one hundred miles to the next waterhole, nor chase flighty gazelles at break-neck speed.

The comparatively small in numbers Greek cavalry, lacking the advantageous shock tactics of the Asian hordes, had to rely on single combat techniques. This necessity combined with the ability to recognise the laws of nature and realise the horse's conformation and its potential development, initiated the art of riding and training which has survived more than two and a half thousand years and is now generally known and unfortunately very often misunderstood as dressage.

The Statesman and General Xenophon wrote the first known book on training and riding in 400 B.C. The ideas and rules he put down are still followed in the Haute Ecole and still are (or should be) the standard rules in training the horse in whatever phase of riding the horse is planned to take part in the end: Haute Ecole, record jumping or cutting out cattle.

Since Xenophon, the art of riding has come a long way. It was carried forth by great masters, adopted by groups of people as their national inheritance.

In the middle ages the art of riding developed to its highest standard. The horseman found it necessary to put his horse into pirouettes, levades and curbettes to survive in battle and in society. Even after the armour was discarded the cavalier's ability to work his mount in all movements of the Haute Ecole "reasonably and with manners" was a must.

Riding masters then held the social esteem and rank of today's physicists.

The development of more accurate firearms made Haute Ecole obsolete for the mounted warrior, although cavalry leaders and instructors still maintain rightly that the trooper on a well trained horse has a better chance of survival than the in-the-stirrup standing rider on an unmanageable rocket.

School movements on and above the ground became useless for military purposes. But there always are and will be people who have an acute sense for beauty and the urge to put impressions and feelings into concrete forms: artists keep the Haute Ecole alive.

What distinguishes the master of riding from any other creative artist is, that his medium is a living being whose physical conformation *and* functions and mental qualities like happiness, pain, joy, fatigue or sorrow have to be considered and worked with. Moreover the master of Haute Ecole has to be mentally *and* physically near perfect.

This probably explains why we have more painters, sculptors, composers or writers than true masters of horsemanship. The difference between the Haute Ecole (or the art of riding) and ordinary field riding is that nothing can be said about the former, only felt. Field riding can be learned by anyone, like darning socks or designing a wallpaper.

But how to express a mood or atmosphere (already here we lack the words to describe it) through a painting, composition or the movement of a living being, as ballet or Haute Ecole can only in the very early beginning be taught and learned: i.e. the manipulation of necessary instruments as the brush, the alphabet, the reins.

The presentation of the objet d'art itself is a mystery and cannot be explained. Nor can it really be explained what makes the artist. Some masters I had the pleasure and privilege to study, seem to have started off with training for a certain purpose like record jumping, polo, cattle work or just ordinary field training, but did, aiming for perfection, during the process get so involved, forgetting time and purpose, that they found themselves putting their mounts through passages and curbettes before they realised what really happened.

As there is no end to the road to perfection, there is no end to training, and the horse who, during the process of training, one day offers his rider a few tentative passage steps, clearly is the best judge as to who is and what makes a master.

After this little excursion into the world of art, let us consider the practical side of Xenophon's training and what its advantages are to us, today.

We are, in a way, in a similar position to the early Greeks, speed is only required in short bursts (polo, cattle work).

Long distances have been taken care of by cars and planes. Even the endurance required at Military competitions is little, compared to the every day performance of Genghis Khan's messengers.

We can only profit by training, i.e. making the whole horse work and function in harmony, preparing it for easier efficiency and happier, longer life through gymnastic exercises.

Some horsemen recognise this and act accordingly. Out of this knowledge Military competitions (One and Three Day Events) were born. It is no accident that the dressage is the first phase.

The idea was to prove that horses well prepared by gymnastic training (dressage) have great advantage against the raw horses who function only on part of their apparatus which must under the double strain break down sooner or later, more often earlier.

What is more, being at least partly constrained bodily, the mind can't be of a happy disposition, nor the rider have a comfortable enjoyable ride. International big-shots in showjumping of lasting fame spend a considerable amount of time on basic training before beginning to jump. It definitely seems to pay dividends in the long run.

The Spaniards took both methods to the Americas. The noble Hidalgos, and the better part of the cavalry followed in Xenophon's tracks as their conditions and requirements were similar, but the Moors had left behind not only some excellent horses, their style of riding, too, had left its mark.

It found its way to the Gauchos of the Argentine pampas. We can now very clearly follow the way of timely and territorial progress from the Mongols via Turkmenistan, Arabia, North Africa to Iberia and Argentina.

Xenophon's theory and its practical application progressed via Rome to the whole of Europe and the Spaniards took it to the then much more extensive Mexico. The descendants of those Spanish Nobles, the Charros and their Vaqueros still train their horses to the rules of the classical art of riding.

From Peru to South California riders realise that it is essential for a good cattle horse to be supple, unconstrained, agile, quick to respond, ready to move anywhere, any time and be capable to move fast suddenly, to endure a long day's work and be comfortable for the rider. This all can only be achieved by strengthening through exercises and flexing the haunches and enlightening the forehand to an, in most cases, unbelievable degree. Some of these

Charros and Vaqueros seem to ride their mounts on the hindlegs alone with none or very little rein aids and both horse and rider seem to enjoy it immensely. An interesting comparison is that the Mexican Vaquero does not change horses all day. The Gaucho uses up three and often four horses a day. It certainly is a spectacle to any horseman's delight to see these Charros promenade their horses at Sunday afternoons on the Plaza.

There are many school movements executed on and above the ground and the levades, lancades, flying changes, pirouettes, passages and curbettes become the more elaborate the prettier the nearby Donnas and senoritas are.

Thanks to the classical training, reins and spurs are no longer necessary, or very little, though they are always present in great beauty and magnificent workmanship.

Horse and rider know they can do a perfect job during the week after cattle, easily, and on Sunday they enjoy themselves immensely making a play of it. Except for the masters of the art of Haute Ecole I cannot see any better horsemanship anywhere or anyhow.

Though I am no authority on this subject allow me to air my view on the so-called English Hunting Style. I don't think there really is an English Hunting Style. The huntsman after hounds has of course developed a natural and appropriate way following etiquette and equestrian requirements. He has no intention to cut out cattle nor to produce an objet d'art. He rides after hounds and does it well. There are of course, those odd ones who ride with their

Not spectacular, but happy and harmonious

seat on the cantle of the saddle and their legs thrust forward, the only contact with horse being the reins and as such making up in strength for the other missing aids.

But this is not the English Hunting Style. It is a degeneration of the crotch seat of the Renaissance. The English Hunting Seat is the Italian forward seat in a mitigated form. It is for this purpose the only possible one. But I do believe there is plenty of room for improvement as far as training is concerned.

Master G. Steinbrecht said: "If the English horse breeder, being the best in Europe, would improve his riding and training to the same standard, he would be impossible to beat in horsemanship".

There is a growing interest in dressage in Britain with extraordinary results. But unfortunately dressage seems to be regarded as a sort of specialty rather than what it really is, or ought to be; basic gymnastic exercise as preparation for greater efficiency and well-being.

I will not try to persuade any rider to accept one or the other line of thought. But I like to ask anyone interested enough, to get *all* the facts before deciding. One must have galloped with the Cossacks over the Steppes, sat out a piaffe in the Vienna Riding School, seen the Vaqueros working cattle and watched these Italian wizards train their horses to jump seven to eight feet to really get some idea what riding can mean and what a wide field it comprises. The decision is with the individual and will greatly be influenced by personal talents and traits.

But whatever it will be, one must go all the way to make a job of it (nothing is more detestable than luke-warm tea), and let us never forget that whatever the end results, sport, art or work, they all grow from the same root: gymnastic training.

Art

WHAT distinguishes the master of the Vienna Riding School from any other rider is his capacity as an artist.

What is art? Art is in my opinion the ability to express a mood, an idea, a thought—any impression—through a medium.

The painter uses pigments, the sculptor stone, the composer sound. The difference between the mason and the sculptor is that the latter brings his stone to life, making it present an atmosphere to be perceived by anybody who cares to see it.

The mason's craftsmanship on the other hand turns the stone into an object of beauty in itself—no more. Skill, experience and knowledge are required by both, the craftsman and the artist.

Quality and perfection must not necessarily be a distinguishing factor between art and craft. But to convey a thought through his work is the artist's privilege alone.

The riding master's medium differs greatly from any other artist's; it is a living being, an animal that breathes, feels and has its own brains to think with.

Piaffe

An animal that can be depressed, happy, over-joyous or frightened. An animal that is a self-contained system in itself, perfectly capable to deal with life on its own.

The artist's requirements are evidently great—first of all in skill. The horse has to be prepared through systemic training to become an efficient instrument in good working order.

Then to produce an objet d'art the master has to tune in to his medium's system to provide for the necessary co-operation and form a partnership that

Passage at liberty . . .

. . . and under the rider

approaches the one system status to produce the work of art. Horse and rider are co-artists, co-media and represent the objet d'art, the model being the foal in the paddock.

There is a close resemblance to the mural painters of the renaissance. They too, had to be masons to prepare the work, chemists to make the paints, scholars to study the subject well enough to comprehend its deeper meaning and convert this meaning with skill into the objet d'art, the mural.

But these master painters did not have to deal with a living creature either and this very fact might well be the reason for masters of the art of riding, rarely if ever, reaching the number of artists in other fields. But this assumption is purely hypothetic as the riding master's product is no lasting one.

The objet d'art's very existence is terminated as the rider dismounts. Moreover there are, I am convinced, numerous unknown artists working to their own enjoyment and not caring to exhibit.

Fortunately we always had, throughout history, outstanding personalities who with their example kept this art from disappearing and handed it down to us. It was not always easy. But even the invention of gunpowder and the industrial revolution could only drive it underground—and this for not very long.

The masters of the Spanish Riding School are the last link of the chain that reaches back to Xenophon. We are grateful to this prominent institution in Vienna and its excellent riders for preserving us the old art in its highest form. We are grateful to these riders for providing us with the example to all horsemanship.

The *Amazone*

A GREAT deal has been said and written about the lady rider. Opinions vary greatly, as a result of the critic's disposition rather than the lady in question's capability.

One might reason that a woman's natural and instinctive pre-occupation with her appearance is a severe handicap in the fine art of riding, as it must hamper mental contact between rider and horse and this might very well be the reason for the fact that we see so very few women performing a truly classic piaffe or passage.

On the other hand women are naturally gifted with qualities essential to good riding, characteristics that are basically foreign or undeveloped in men. A woman is generally more sensitive and many a woman rider will put a he-man to shame by being able to handle a notorious "puller" easily by means of feel and sensitive hands, or get along well with difficult horses through understanding.

Her intuitions will help the woman rider greatly—until a male instructor tells her to forget it. The woman who uses her power of intuition to establish contact with her horse will indeed easily surpass her male counterpart, who has to translate thought into human language—into horse language—into reactions and back until, after years of tedious endeavours to improve this inefficient system, he develops automatically and subconsciously his intuition to a degree where he can use it as a medium for communications with his horse; even then he will deny such "mystics" and attribute his progress to his learnedness.

The typical female attitude of passivity in the face of difficulties and problems is the very means to overcome problems at any stage of training, as paradox as it might sound. To force the issue means, as any woman knows, disaster or at least setbacks.

The best motive should rather be: surrender dominance and purposeful action in favour of spiritual and physical one-ness.

In effect, do your best towards the horse, as a result the horse will present you with whatever you have been dreaming about. In other words: not the working towards a piaffe will eventually produce a piaffe but a deep seat and uninterrupted communication with the horse in the trot and its transitions will automatically eventuate in a true classic piaffe.

Generally speaking, a woman will subscribe to this line of thinking more readily than a man and the advantage is subsequently hers. In regard to the deep seat a woman might have difficulties to place her leg flat on the saddle. A rolling thigh muscle between the femur and saddle causes an unstable seat, pushes the knee off the horse and turns the toes out.

But the remedy is easy, simply by pulling the thigh muscle back and out from between the femur and saddle, and simultaneously, to keep them there, pushing the heels down and out and the seat forward against the withers.

In the early stages of training the rider might have to stop and re-arrange her seat more frequently, but eventually the deep classic seat will become her natural one and then only the lady's urge to look in the mirror could be a slight handicap on the way to mastership of classic art of riding.

Hilaire Belloc's *Waterbeetle*:

> If she ever stopped to think
> of how she did it, she would sink.

In the stables

THE HORSE is our friend and should be treated as such. I loathe those who endlessly talk to and pet their horses as much as those who abuse them. Mutual enjoyment at work and play, yes; fussing, no; certainly not at feeding time.

Who wants to be patted on the head while having his dinner? It only irritates. Fussing about and other general disturbances at feeding time are annoying to the horse and are one of the main causes of colic. Titbits of sugar are a dirty trick to make the animal dependent, it reminds me of dope peddling. Carrots, stale bread, or apples on the other hand are good food stuffs and just as much liked.

The horse should be fed two hours before work, the time it takes to digest whole oats. A full stomach tends to make the horse sluggish, Nature's safeguard against over-straining the heart. Straight after work we offer our friend something it likes very much with a high nutritional value, such as fresh bread or carrots.

This is a very much appreciated way of saying "thank you".

Moreover, as there always will in systematic training be certain parts of the horse under extreme strain (for example the muscles and bands of the haunches) the accute deficiency there will draw more effectively, replenishments to these very points.

Oats always were and will be the number one energy food for working horses, with barley a close second. They should be fed whole whenever a horse has no trouble chewing and digesting them in a one: one chaff mixture (volume, not weight). Good, sound, well cured, sweet-smelling meadow hay should go with every meal of which there should be three, or better four, as evenly as possible distributed over the twenty-four hour day.

The biggest meal is fed in the evening when the animal has peace and quiet to eat and digest. Freshly cut legumes, preferably lucerne in small portions throughout the day are of the greatest benefit to health and well-being. The lucerne plant originated in Media (Medic) the now northern Persia and parts of Turkmenstan where still the very best horses come from.

The Persians called it Aspest—horse fodder, and with the horses it reached Arabia and the Mediterranean where the Arabs called it alfalfa—the best of fodder. The very high protein and mineral content, especially phosphorus and calcium make it indeed the best of fodders—definitely so for growing and working animals.

Fresh, cool water is essential. The ideal being water in which trout would live happily. If rain water is used mineral salt licks must be made available. Any other foodstuffs or substitutes are unnecessary. Wet mashes belong in the pig-fattening business; our noble friends of the steppes should not be degraded to such mess. Whenever in doubt it is easy to imagine what our horse would choose at liberty. The horse's natural instinct is the best judge as to its requirements as long as it has not been conditioned to unnatural "treats".

I once knew a horse who was extremely keen on sausages, preferably fried and piping hot. But this was a victim of man's love for sensationalism which should never creep into stable nor riding arena. There are scores of horse owners who excel themselves in concocting the most intricate food rations.

The only practical advantage this "scientific" approach offers is to satisfy those people's self esteem. The frequent claims of bran being a necessary stimulant to bowel movement is unfounded. If a horse is healthy, treated calmly and with no fuss, has twenty-four hour access to water, given time to eat and digest and is given some fresh green feed daily, six-ten lbs of oats with chaff, good meadow hay unlimited, thirty-forty lbs fresh lucerne (in winter ten lbs lucerne hay instead) and three-five lbs of carrots will take care of the horse's needs under any training conditions —except racing of course.

The green lucerne will *not* cause colic if given in small lots and if the horse is left to eat it unhurriedly.

In localities where the foodstuffs are grown on deficient soils minerals might have to be added to the diet. But it is really simpler and safer to correct the nutrition level in paddock and field than in the feed room. Generous supply of calcium, phosphorus and nitrogen to the soils that produce pasture, oats and lucerne is of great importance to the health of our horse and a 99 % assurance against serious deficiencies; a possible lack in one plant will be compensated for by another's abundance.

The overlapping of deficiencies–if any–and abundance in the various plants which make up the horse's food supply guarantees an overall balanced diet.

The ideal accommodation for a horse in training is a wooden rail yard with an open fronted stall attached to it, where the horse may go in or out as it pleases. The set-up should face away from the prevailing rough weather. One or two shade trees provide comfort in hot summer days.

Needless to say the ground must be well drained and if possible, sandy. Pleasant surroundings help greatly to make our horse happy and contented. It wants to see what is going on and an unobstructed view helps to satisfy its curiosity.

Half a day's grazing and playing in a good paddock only helps the training. What greater joy can there be for our horse than a free gallop, a few bucks and a roll, peaceful grazing, sunshine and freedom from worries. A contented horse is a happy one and a happy horse causes few if any difficulties in training.

The purpose of grooming is to keep the horse clean and happy, all it amounts to is to brush out the itching dandruff, wash out eyes, nostrils, mouth etc and occasionally trim the hooves. A healthy well-fed horse does not have to be shoe-shined.

The so-often-claimed advantages of the skin massage with the brush might have their importance with those pitiful creatures who have to spend their lives in stables. We let wind and an occasional swim do the job.

Making our horse comfortable *after* the work is where the emphasis of grooming must be. Offering refreshment in form of a few carrots or some fresh lucerne. Sponging the face, between the legs and the girth positions, rubbing down with handfuls of hay (whether the coat is wet or not) providing for feed and water *before* we light that cigarette or go to dinner.

This rubbing down with hay is the best skin and coat care there is. The coat must be warm (or hot), the hands with a little hay in each, move fast but lightly with the hair, beginning behind the ears, working towards the tail. It combines massage, cleaning and polishing and is the speediest of all grooming methods. Should the horse want to roll, let it, by all means—it is the natural reaction of a warm horse and shows its health, fitness and well-being.

We finish off by scraping out the hoofs (hoof fat prevents brittleness of the horn and makes the farrier's job a lot easier) and brushing out the tail and mane. "Thank you my friend, are you happy now?" That is all, no fuss.

It is unkind to let a horse stand and wait. It is extremely inconsiderate to bring a horse in dripping wet, in fact it proves the absence of any horsemanship. A horse can do its very best without being driven to a lather. A horse that has never been abused will, when the occasion arises, willingly sacrifice itself, and the rider must treat it as such, a sacrifice.

Psychology

ANIMAL psychology as a science has undoubtedly its place—in the lecture hall—but not in the riding arena. Psychology necessitates analysing which puts it in direct opposition to our "horse-rider-one-unit" concept.

The most cunningly devised experiments supposedly leading to conclusions are based on insufficient data to begin with.

This is not a simple equation as $A+B=C$; the possibilities and their combinations are infinite and mostly unknown. Conclusion drawn from incomplete statistics must result in contortions or shallow generalisations. Whatever horse psychology has been presented to us so far has only convinced me of its erroneous ways and misleading results.

The animal's psyche is entirely ignored. What psychologists experiment with largely is pure mechanics, for example the image on the eye's retina is clearly demonstrated and certain body functions as a result of this given image predicted. But how the mind interprets and reacts and what role the psyche has within this process is anybody's guess.

Infinite theories can be established in regard to the pysche of which none must necessarily be the truth. It seems an utter waste of time and energy to dissect, examine and tag numerous bits and pieces, throw them on a heap and proclaim this conglomeration to be the true object under observation, because "the angle of slope measures 47·5 degrees". Much better results are obtained in less time by approaching the subject direct and as a whole.

It is much simpler than generally thought to establish direct mental contact with the animal. Anyone undoubtedly perceives the first glimpse of the inside story when approaching a green unbroken youngster in the paddock, oats in out-stretched hand, the halter concealed behind one's back. If one's gaze is diffused over the whole horse ("don't look in his eyes") one cannot help getting a notion of the forces that pull and push the animal, inbred fright, curiosity, distrust (how justified!), greed for food, resignation to the unavoidable etc.

The reason why natural riders are mostly one jump ahead of this scientific-approach-fellow is, I am convinced, that the former is in almost constant subconscious contact with the animal—the invisible foundation of all horsemanship without which the upper structure, the constant physical contact, can only be a portentous affair, temporary, exhibitionistic and hazardous.

We all agree, more or less grudgingly about the existence of the undefined something which is part of any phenomenon, functions and very existence of life. It can only be seen and felt by its actions and it is easily recognised by what it does—never by what it is. To anyone attempting to put his finger on it, it will disappear behind a curtain of secrecy. To master these powerful forces man describes them—according to his temperament—in terms of art, religion or simply predesigned functions of a pure euclidean world.

None of these concepts must necessarily be right nor is it very likely anybody will ever know the truth. The best we can do is to recognise this certain something by its actions, accept them and try to co-ordinate our own ways with it.

The primary stumbling block on the road to art, religious belief, is in fact man's superiority. Considering himself the crown of creation, he sees the world and its phenomena as a chess board which automatically entitles him to move figures, his opponent being *nature*. It is futile to attempt to master all games (as he does not even know of the existence of many of them) or to influence the progress of them.

In equestrian terms this means that the rider cannot possibly know and be in command of all the physical functions and mental conditions. He can only "feel" them and experience them subconsciously by surrendering dominance over the subject in favour to unison with it.

Equipment

THE LOWEST point in the saddle, everyone agrees, should be in the middle between pommel and cantle. But how many saddles fulfil this simple requirement? It is impossible to go into and maintain the forward-driving seat in a backwards-sloping saddle. In these idiotic contraptions the rider's seatbones slide back, legs go forward away from the horse. Result is the Australian stockman seat in which the only contact with the horse is by means of the reins. It is beyond my understanding why it should be more effort and expense to make saddles with their deepest part in the centre. A little consideration and how much effort and misery to horses and riders alike could be eliminated!

Another incomprehensible fact is the extensive length of saddles. A properly-sitting rider usually shows one to two hand-breadths of leather behind his posterior. Why? In addition to the waste of material this excess stern structure is of no value to anyone. In fact it puts pressure on the very part of the horse's back that ought to be free and which I certainly would not like to be continuously pressed and bumped on. The rider of average build is in the majority. Could not oversized people have oversize saddles as is the rule in the garment trade?

No words are needed about the padding. Overstuffed easy chairs are out. The less material between rider and horse the better. Auxiliary reins are no means to training nor do they provide a remedy to bad riding. A martingale might protect a hurdling jockey's nose from disfiguration but even this is doubtful because if adjusted so as not to interfere with rein aids it does not function as designed anyway. Running reins are like pure democracy. The very few people who can handle them with advantage—do not need them. This little wisdom applies to all additional gear, including the whip. The cases where a whip should not have been applied are much more numerous than the rare occurrence of a "missed" whip aid. The logical conclusion is to leave the thing to mould in the tackroom. In the hand of a master—yes. But then again, one rarely sees a master using it. Spurs? By all means—IF the rider is convinced beyond any doubt that they are not boosters for speed but emergency airbrakes and should only be used as such, i.e. to bring the hindlegs forward under the mass—in an emergency!

So it is apparent that the only equipment we need for all training from the first tentative, cramped steps to the levade consists of simple bridle, possibly a cavesson, and a saddle to save our skin. And even this is of secondary importance and after, first of all, the love for the horse, an enormous amount of patience, the ability to feel and willingness to integrate.

Bits

In contrast to the general belief I am convinced that the curb is a less severe bit than the snaffle. In fact, the longer the side levers the more gentle the curb becomes.

Flexibility and elasticity are very important factors for all training and riding and the levers of the curb provide the rider with these important means.

The experienced rider recognises the great help of the "feathering" curb. Only a well balanced horse can of course be ridden on the curb with advantage. The horse that carries itself on the forehand will overbend and therefore enlighten its hindquarters even more. The lack of skill has made the curb unpopular because direct aids cannot be given through a curb, nor can a horse be steered, and every other possible aid has to be applied, mainly the forward-driving seat, before an aid through the curb will be answered.

The snaffle on the other hand, though just as severe if pulled directly can be applied effectively before the horse is balanced, here direct rein aids are possible without doing any obvious damage.

A great amount of pull can be put on the snaffle reins, before the casual onlooker or, more important, the rider realises the detrimental effects it causes. Unfortunately this increased its popularity.

Concerning gentleness the argument snaffle versus curb is in my opinion in favour of the curb, provided of course, brute force is not applied. The sheering effect of the snaffle on the lower jaw with its joint pressing against the roof of the mouth must be very painful indeed in contrast to the gentle feathering of the curb which cannot possibly cause any pain to the horse, especially if the chain is replaced with a soft strap.

From the training point of view the curb is of immense advantage mainly due to the fact that direct rein aids are not possible; they would only create resistance, overbending or stargazing.

To benefit from the advantages of the curb the horse *must* be ridden from behind, the balance must be perfect and appropriate to the movement, with the hindlegs carrying their share of the mass.

Rein aids then become the fingertip control, gently feathering, sensitive to the slightest deviation of balance. The ampere-meter, so to speak, of a current created by the rider's forward-driving seat and the horse's impulsion. It is obvious that the direct acting snaffle can never be the instrument for such perfection.

The Spanish snaffle is the only other bit, apart from snaffle and curb, that I had practical experience with. This bit is quite advantageous in the early stages of training. It is practically a curb without levers and therefore direct rein aids can be applied.

I personally, and my horses, give the Spanish snaffle definite preference to the ordinary snaffle as it does not sheer the lower jaw nor press against the roof of the mouth.

I am no authority on any other type of bit, though there are dozens of versions, and though one or the other might be very useful in certain circumstances let us not forget it is the hands that are important, not the shape of the bit.

Good hands (undetachable from the good seat) will do a good job with any bit. On the other hand, no bit, of whatever shape it might be and whatever ingenious function it was designed for, can ever be a substitute for bad hands. Let me quote an old master on this subject: the less cunningly designed devices and the fewer assisting instruments, the closer to life and true art. I cannot think of anything better to say.

The old masters used the cavesson to begin with and, though their horses were bitted with a curb to get them used to the feel of it, all rein aids were given by the cavesson directly to the nose bone. The results were spectacular.

Technically, any rein aids to the upper jaw (nose bone) influence the stretcher muscles of the neck, presupposedly, of course, the horse is "ridden forward" and forward impulsion is sufficient to provide the necessary contact with the reins. On the other hand, a bit, any bit, will act on the lower jaw exclusively, to which the horse's natural reaction is to keep his mouth shut, i.e. contracting for a start two muscles to do so. These two contracted muscles will affect others like a contagious disease, speeded up by clumsy riders' constant "corrective rein aids" till the miserable "trainer" feels like sitting astride a log in water.

Whoever tries the cavesson method will be surprised to find that even the most vigorous and stormy horse can be controlled easily without a bit, solely with rein aids direct to the nose bone.

The explanation is simple; annoyance and pain-causing resistance are eliminated. The old masters recognised this and rode their horses happily, and when they eventually discarded the cavesson as obsolete they found the curb too was barely necessary for so featherlight had the contact become that the weight of the reins alone maintained it perfectly.

A compromise between the cavesson and the bit is the drop nose band, but it can never be more than a compromise.

And with all this talk about bits I am convinced the best bit is no bit at all, but if we do use one let us regard it as a necessary evil and not pay too much attention to it.

What *is* important is the hands, steady and gentle. Rein aids are after all only the interpunctuation after the sentence, that is, after everything during one full stride has been said through all other available aids.

CONCLUSION

THE difference between classic training and schooling is that in training, the horse ridden according to the laws of nature will offer in its own time, as by-products as it were, classic movements.

The closer these movements resemble the foal's frolicking jumps and airs or a youngster's moody expressions in poise and gait the better is the training.

The taught horse's movements on the other hand are unnatural, no matter how impressive they may look, they are outside the law of nature, inferior in efficiency, detrimental to the horse's health and happiness, uncomfortable to the rider.

One of the wisdoms of life is to co-ordinate one's so-called free will with what nature wants us to "will". Is it not only extremely exhausting but downright stupid to battle straight across the stream if one can do it much easier by partly making use of the current for one's progress.

As life itself teaches us, this must not necessarily take longer as the battling never ends once started, with the battler for ever almost in reach of the carrot on the stick but never actually catching it. As in the race between the tortoise and the hare, the rider who goes along with nature will already *be* where the teacher-trainer never quite arrives. The philosophy of surrendering dominance in favour of concord is a good rule for sailing, farming, in fact all life.

We all know seasickness only overtakes the voyager who fights the sea: the farmer who goes along with nature, who lives with the soil for the soil and off the soil, who sees himself part of the soil, will grow the biggest potatoes. The rider who earnestly and sincerely strives to learn from nature what her rules are and what she plans for the future will have a smooth life in the saddle.

He will know that liberty in its true sense can only be achieved by cessation of resistance.

If nature wants horses to express themselves in passages, courbettes and caprioles it would be preposterous to teach them movements concocted by halfwits.

Our ideal: the horse-rider-one-unit can only be achieved by fusion, never by fission. Rather than forming, altering and correcting let us recognise, accept, absorb and help.

But this has been said long ago, much better and more precisely.

What do we want to do with the world? It is made, and nature has thought of everything.

C. E. EDKINS